Welcome,
LEGO
fans!

LEGO® minifigures show you the world in a unique non-fiction programme.

This reader is part of a programme of LEGO® non-fiction books, with something for all the family, at every age and stage.
LEGO non-fiction books have amazing facts, beautiful real-world photos, and minifigures everywhere, leading the fun and discovery.

To find out about the books in the programme, visit www.scholastic.co.uk

Levelled readers from Scholastic are designed to support your child's efforts to learn how to read at every age and stage.

White level books use a sophisticated narrative voice. They include longer sentences, using commas to separate clauses. Some White level books have longer chapters to encourage reading stamina.

What's bugging you?

BUG OFF!

A LEGO® ADVENTURE IN THE REAL WORLD

by Penelope Arlon
and Tory Gordon-Harris

Get the buzz
on bugs in this book!
Gotta fly!

■SCHOLASTIC

New York Toronto London Auckland
Sydney Mexico City New Delhi Hong Kong

Contents

BUILD IT!

Check out the epic building ideas when you see me!

I've heard there are up to 10 million kinds of insect. I've only spotted one!

3

There are about 200 million bugs for every person on the planet.

BUILD IT!

Build a super-bug. Make sure it has lots of legs and huge wings!

There are lots of types of bug that have never been spotted before ...by anyone!

I want to find bugs that can fly loop-the-loop and even fly backwards! Tally ho!

Who's who?

We use the word "bug" to talk about tiny creatures that live on land. Bugs can be divided into groups. You can often tell which group a bug belongs to by counting its legs. But be quick! Some bugs are fast!

The giant weta cricket is the biggest insect. It is also the most powerful kicker, like me!

Segmented worm: no legs

Mollusk like slugs and snails: no legs

HEARD THIS WORD?

antennae: feelers on some bugs' heads that look like little sticks.

Insect, like ladybirds and ants: 6 legs

Arachnid, like spiders and scorpions: 8 legs

Woodlouse: 14 legs

The tiniest insect is the fairyfly. It's smaller than the dot over this letter i. Sweet!

Centipede and millipede: lots and lots of legs

Some bugs behave badly. They bite! They sting! They carry germs! But most bugs are good guys. They stop our world from being super-smelly. Every day, animals drop lots of poo. The dung beetle makes poo into a ball. It then rolls the ball away to eat or lay its eggs in.

Millions of insects eat up dead leaves and wood on the forest floor. Their poo makes the soil rich for growing plants.

BUILD IT!

Build a big rubbish truck that can help recycle, just like the bugs do!

Why do bees have sticky hair? Because they have honeycombs!

Want an apple for lunch? Thank a bug! Bugs carry pollen from one flower to another. This means that plants can make seeds and fruit. Honey bees sip sweet nectar from flowers. They will use it to make honey. As they sip, pollen sticks to them. They carry the pollen to another flower, where there's more nectar to sip!

pollen: the yellow plant dust that is carried to other plants so that they can produce seeds.

Thank you, bees, for all this yummy honey. It takes thousands of bees to make just one pot of honey!

That's a lot of work! I guess that's where the saying "busy as a bee" comes from! Yikes! I don't think they want to share.

Incredible insects

All insects have three body parts – a head; a thorax with the legs attached; and an abdomen, which is usually the biggest part. They also have three pairs of jointed legs, antennae and some have wings. Insects have all sorts of amazing abilities. Fireflies can light up their bodies. Fleas can jump 150 times their own height!

Pond skaters don't need a boat. They can walk right across water. Their light bodies barely dent the surface.

Insects come in a rainbow of colours. Sometimes their colours say, "I taste gross." Other times they warn, "STAY AWAY!" The brightest bugs are the most dangerous. They are usually poisonous to their predators.

HEARD THIS WORD?

predator: an animal that hunts and eats other animals.

Ancient Egyptians made colourful jewels in the shape of beetles.

I can top that! The ancient Mayans wore LIVE beetles as jewellery.

BUILD IT!

Design and build an insect that is so colourful, it will never be eaten!

Some insects have another way of avoiding predators. They look exactly like the nature around them. They can't be eaten if their enemy can't spot them. They might mimic a stick or a leaf. Can you spot the insects in these pictures?

This caterpillar looks just like bird poo. No one will want a bite of it!

...eight, nine, ten.
Coming, ready
or not!

Tee hee! Fly
Monster will
NEVER spot me
in these flowers.

Oops, you left your
antennae sticking up.
Found you!

The most incredible insects of all live in the forests of North and South America. Thousands of leafcutter ants work together.

They cut and carry small pieces of leaves across the forest floor. Each piece can be 50 times as heavy as the ant carrying it. The ants live in underground nests, where they eat fungus that grows on the chewed leaves.

I spy with my mini-eye... some helpful insects in the garden.

Insects help plants grow and they nibble pests. Take a hike, pests!

Bug babies

There is one thing all insects are good at – making baby insects! Almost all insects lay eggs. They lay them somewhere safe, like under a leaf or in wood. Most insect parents leave their eggs alone and the babies take care of themselves.

Insects often lay their eggs on a leaf so it can be their babies' first meal.

Shield bugs are a bit different. The female lays eggs and then guards them until the nymphs (babies) hatch.

BUILD IT!

Build a submarine so your bug explorers can search for mosquito eggs in the water!

Eggs

Pupa

Larva

Do you love butterflies?
They start life looking very
different. Butterfly eggs hatch
into caterpillars. A caterpillar
eats and eats and eats. It grows
up to 100 times bigger. Then
it becomes a pupa.

Beetles, flies, bees
and ants go through
three stages before they
turn into adults.

HEARD THIS WORD?

pupa: the stage between larva and adult. Some insects build a shell around themselves.

......Butterfly

After weeks or months, the pupa breaks open and a butterfly flies out!

Creeping and crawling

Do you find bugs gross? Or creepy? The bugs that seem the most creepy are often the most incredible. Slugs and snails are bug super-movers. They leave a trail of slimy mucus which helps them move smoothly, even upside down. They are super-strong. Snails can carry up to ten times their own weight!

Did you know slugs have more teeth than sharks? They've got up to 27,000 chompers to rip food into bits.

Snail slime is incredible stuff. Scientists think it can heal our skin.

Let's fix you up, Clumsy Guy. It's slime time for you!

The biggest bug of all time lived about 300 million years ago. It was a kind of millipede. It could grow to be more than 1.8 metres (6 ft long)! Gross!

The Amazonian giant centipede hunts and eats bats!

That's batty!

Nowadays, the biggest millipedes are about 38 cm (15 in). They have two pairs of legs on each body segment. Some have 750 legs!

BUILD IT!

Build a centipede. How many legs does it have?

Centipedes have one pair of legs on each body segment. They also have a pair of fangs to help them hunt other bugs.

If a group of millipedes formed a football team, they would need more than 4,000 pairs of boots!

Octan

In the web

Spiders give some people the creeps. But they are probably the coolest bugs around. All spiders spin silk. Some weave them into beautiful webs. Webs are made to catch insects. Silk is also used to wrap up eggs to keep them safe. One spider even makes a little net that it drops on insects to catch them!

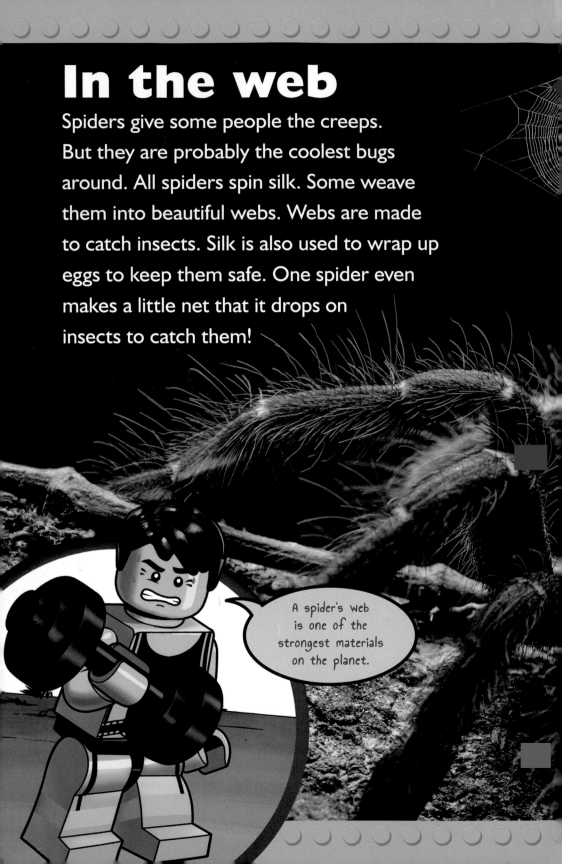

A spider's web is one of the strongest materials on the planet.

Whoa! Where did all these spiders come from?

Relax, my pet spider's eggs have hatched. She laid over 1,000 eggs and there are more to come!

orb weaver

tarantula

It's bugtastic!

It's a minifigure adventure in a bug world!
From all the creepy-crawlies you've just
read about, choose your favourite.
Then build it!

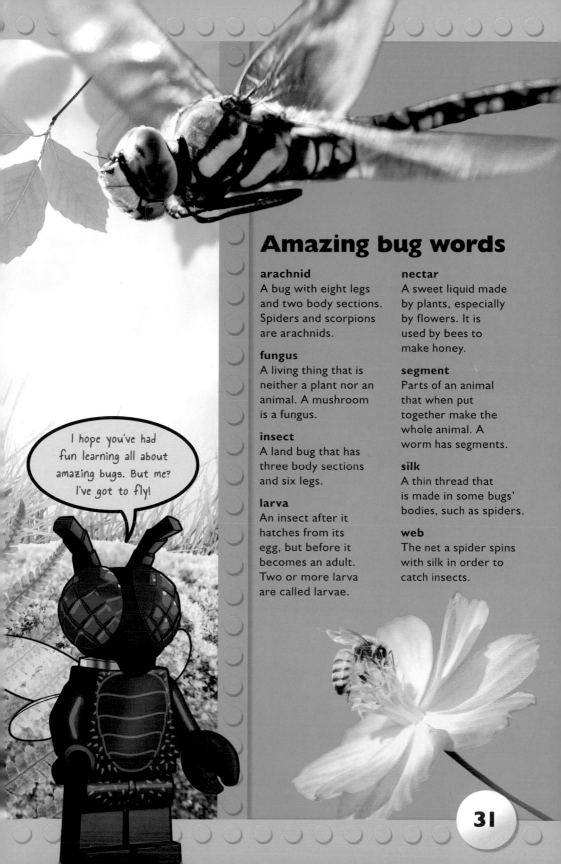

Amazing bug words

arachnid
A bug with eight legs and two body sections. Spiders and scorpions are arachnids.

fungus
A living thing that is neither a plant nor an animal. A mushroom is a fungus.

insect
A land bug that has three body sections and six legs.

larva
An insect after it hatches from its egg, but before it becomes an adult. Two or more larva are called larvae.

nectar
A sweet liquid made by plants, especially by flowers. It is used by bees to make honey.

segment
Parts of an animal that when put together make the whole animal. A worm has segments.

silk
A thin thread that is made in some bugs' bodies, such as spiders.

web
The net a spider spins with silk in order to catch insects.

I hope you've had fun learning all about amazing bugs. But me? I've got to fly!

Index

Credits

For the LEGO Group: Peter Moorby Licensing Coordinator; Heidi K. Jensen Licensing Manager;
Photos ©: cover main: Erik Karits/Alamy Images; cover top left: Miroslaw Kijewski/iStockphoto;
cover top right: GlobalP/iStockphoto; cover, back cover top background: Jason Lugo/iStockphoto;
back cover ladybugs: Alexandr Pakhnyushchyy/iStockphoto; 1: YapAhock/Shutterstock, Inc.; 2-3
moss: finallast/iStockphoto; 2-3 background: Andreealonascu/iStockphoto; 3 top leaves: Borut
Trdina/iStockphoto; 3 main: GlobalP/iStockphoto; 4 left: Super Prin/Shutterstock, Inc.; 4-5
background: Laura Pashkevich/Shutterstock, Inc.; 4 right: Antagain/iStockphoto; 5 top: gui00878/
iStockphoto; 5 center left: Warayoo/iStockphoto; 5 center right: macroworld/iStockphoto; 6
bottom: wasantistock/iStockphoto; 6 top right, 7 top left: Valentina Razumova/Shutterstock, Inc.;
7 center left: Lusoimages/iStockphoto; 7 center: Artem Povarov/iStockphoto; 7 center right top:
Antagain/iStockphoto; 7 center right bottom: Antagain/iStockphoto; 7 bottom right: anatchant/
iStockphoto; 8-9 background: pilotL39/iStockphoto; 8-9 moss: Alexander Dunkel/iStockphoto; 8
main: Henrik Larsson/Shutterstock, Inc.; 9 mushrooms: unrestedm/iStockphoto; 9 main: Four
Oaks/Shutterstock, Inc.; 10-11 top background: StudioSmart/Shutterstock, Inc.; 10 bottom left:
Pan Xunbin/Shutterstock, Inc.; 10-11 main: Protasov AN/Shutterstock, Inc.; 12-13: karthik
photography/Getty Images; 14-15 background: IakovKalinin/iStockphoto; 14 top left: BUFOTO/
Shutterstock, Inc.; 14 top right: Lisa Thornberg/iStockphoto; 14 center right: Antagain/
iStockphoto; 15 top left: Antagain/iStockphoto; 15 center left: LPETTET/iStockphoto; 15 bottom
left: YapAhock/Shutterstock, Inc.; 15 center right: Subbotina Anna/Shutterstock, Inc.; 15 bottom
right: Triduza/iStockphoto; 15 bottom center: arlindo71/iStockphoto; 16 left: Pete Oxford/Getty
Images; 16 bottom right: Leeman/iStockphoto; 16 top right: Ch'ien Lee/Getty Images; 17 bottom
left: Fabien Monteil/Shutterstock, Inc.; 17 bottom right: Achim Prill/iStockphoto; 18 left:
Genevieve Vallee/Alamy Images; 18-19 background: Thomas Marent/Getty Images; 20 top left
black eggs: Nik Br/Shutterstock, Inc.; 20 top left pink eggs: SIMON SHIM/Shutterstock, Inc.;
20-21 main: mikroman6/Getty Images; 21 bottom: Nik Br/Shutterstock, Inc.; 22-23 main: abzerit/
iStockphoto; 22 top left leaf: phittavas/iStockphoto; 22 top left larva: Al Braunworth/iStockphoto;
22 top left eggs: Peter Waters/Shutterstock, Inc.; 22 top right, 23 top left:
StevenRussellSmithPhotos/Shutterstock, Inc.; 24-25 background: dragnab/iStockphoto; 24 left:
AndreyTarakanov/Shutterstock, Inc.; 24-25 bottom: Andyworks/iStockphoto; 25 top right: Kativ/
iStockphoto; 25 top left: Nailia Schwarz/Shutterstock, Inc.; 26 top left: THPStock/iStockphoto;
26-27 main: Jolkesky/iStockphoto; 26-27 bottom background: Andreealonascu/iStockphoto;
26-27 bottom: tinnapong/iStockphoto; 28-29 main: Ch'ien Lee/Getty Images; 29 top left:
magnetix/Shutterstock, Inc.; 29 center left: Brandon Alms/Shutterstock, Inc.; 30-31 top
background: Borut Trdina/iStockphoto; 30 right ferns: Elena Elisseeva/iStockphoto; 30 bottom
left: ConstantinCornel/iStockphoto; 30-31 center background: Andreealonascu/iStockphoto;
30-31 bottom background: finallast/iStockphoto; 30 left ferns: J.Y. Loke/Shutterstock, Inc.;
31 top: gui00878/iStockphoto; 31 bottom right: Tarbell Studio Photo/Shutterstock, Inc.; 32
background: Andreealonascu/iStockphoto.
All LEGO illustrations by Paul Lee and Sean Wang

> Thanks to all the amazing bugs we met on our big, bugtastic adventure.

Scholastic Children's Books,
Euston House,
24 Eversholt Street,
London NW1 1DB, UK

A division of Scholastic Ltd

London ~ New York ~ Toronto ~ Sydney ~ Auckland
Mexico City ~ New Delhi ~ Hong Kong

This book was first published in the US in 2017 by Scholastic Inc.
Published in the UK by Scholastic Ltd, 2017

ISBN 978 1407 17234 7